FIRST-PERSON ACTION ESPORTS

THE COMPETITIVE GAMING WORLD OF OVERWATCH, COUNTER-STRIKE, AND MORE!

by Thomas Kingsley Troupe

CAPSTONE PRESS
a capstone imprint

Edge Books are published by Capstone Press,
1710 Roe Crest Drive, North Mankato, Minnesota 56003
www.capstonepub.com

Library of Congress Cataloging-in-Publication Data
Names: Troupe, Thomas Kingsley, author.
Title: First-person action esports : the competitive gaming world of Overwatch,
    Counter-strike, and more! / by Thomas Kingsley Troupe.
Description: North Mankato, Minnesota : Capstone Press, 2020. | Series: Edge
    books. Wide world of esports | Includes bibliographical references and
    index. | Audience: Age 8–14. | Audience: Grade 4 to 6.
Identifiers: LCCN 2019005959 (print) | LCCN 2019006608 (ebook) |
    ISBN 9781543573657 (eBook PDF) | ISBN 9781543573534 (library binding) |
    ISBN 9781543574524 (paperback)
Subjects: LCSH: Video games—Competitions—Juvenile literature. | Video
    gamers—Juvenile literature.
Classification: LCC GV1469.3 (ebook) | LCC GV1469.3 .T77 2020 (print) |
    DDC 794.8—dc23
LC record available at https://lccn.loc.gov/2019005959

Summary: Describes professional video gaming leagues and game tournaments
including *Overwatch, Counter-Strike: Global Offensive, Call of Duty*, and more.

Editorial Credits
Aaron Sautter, editor; Kyle Grenz, designer; Tracy Cummins, media researcher;
    Laura Manthe, production specialist

Photo Credits
Alamy: Erik Tham, 14-15; AP Images: Spencer Green, 20; Getty Images:
Caiaimage, 24, CHANDAN KHANNA/AFP, 22, Christian Petersen, 10-11,
DAVID MCNEW/AFP, 6-7, 12-13, Hannah Smith/ESPAT Media, 18, Joe Scarnici,
5, Mirrorpix, 9, Norbert Barczyk/ PressFocus/MB Media, 17, Robert Reiners,
27; Shutterstock: EKKAPHAN CHIMPALEE, Design Element, Eky Studio,
Design Element, glazok90, Design Element, Gorodenkoff, 4, JJFarq, 29, Maryna
Kulchytska, Design Element, Phojai Phanpanya, Design Element, Roman
Kosolapov, Cover Top Left, 26, Rvector, Design Element, Simikov, Cover Top
Right; Wikimedia/Flickr/Joi Ito, 8

Printed in the United States of America.
PA70

Table of Contents

First-Person Frenzy

Laser bolts zing overhead. One strikes the teammate behind you. You dive behind the nearby statue for cover. Luckily, your team's **sniper** takes out an enemy from above, saving your neck. As you move in to secure the zone, a grenade explodes near you. The blast staggers you back and knocks away some of your health.

sniper—a soldier trained to shoot at long-distance targets from a hidden place

4

As you recover, a swarm of enemies streams into the courtyard. They open fire, clipping you in the shoulder. You leap into the air and blast away as gunfire tears up the ground beneath your feet. When you land, enemies quickly close in to try and retake the zone. You throw down an energy shield to block their progress. Thankfully, your team's **medic** heals your wounds during the break in the action. You'll have to be ready for the final showdown soon.

medic—a soldier trained to give medical help in an emergency or during a battle

Team Canada and Team Australia compete in the Overwatch World Cup at BlizzCon 2017 in Anaheim, California.

OVERWATCH

AUSTRALIA

Arena Action

The crowd around you explodes into cheers and applause. You dodge enemy fire and blast away at the other team's ranks. Your teammates sit at monitors near you, their controllers gripped in their hands. All six of you have worked hard at the tournament to reach these final moments. One bad move could mean the difference between victory and defeat!

Gamers were once considered lazy people who spent all day in front of TVs or computer screens. But recently esports, or competitive electronic sports, have exploded in popularity. Thousands of fans pack arenas to cheer on their favorite players. Highly skilled gamers can become professionals and earn a lot of money playing games. In fact, some are nearly as famous and well paid as any professional athletes. In the wide world of esports, the future is now!

Esport tournaments often draw huge crowds of gaming fans to watch pro gamers compete for big prizes.

Fun Fact

Esports fans don't need to go to an arena to watch their favorite games and players. Millions of fans around the world watch live tournaments on the internet. Some competitions are even broadcast on ESPN just like traditional sports.

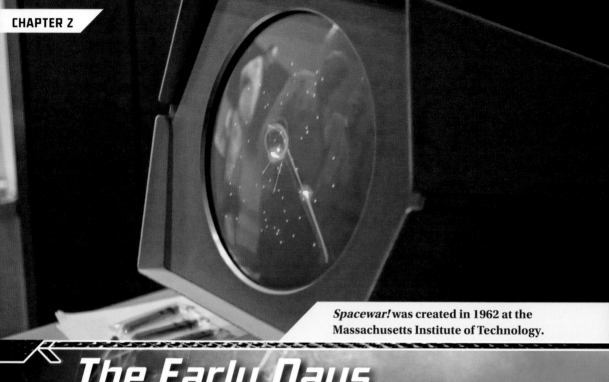

CHAPTER 2

Spacewar! was created in 1962 at the Massachusetts Institute of Technology.

The Early Days of Esports

Classic Competitions

Today's video game competitions are huge events. But video game competitions started out much smaller. In 1972 at Stanford University's AI (Artificial Intelligence) Labs, students were invited to compete in the first Intergalactic Spacewar Olympics. It was the first-ever competitive video game tournament. *Spacewar!* had a simple concept. Players controlled various small spaceships and fired weapons to destroy their opponent.

As video games became more popular, competitions began to grow. In 1980 the Atari video game company held a tournament for one of its most popular games. Over 10,000 players competed in the 1980 Space Invaders Championship. It was the biggest video game event to that time. But it wouldn't be long before even bigger gaming competitions began to take place.

Fun Fact

The winner of the Intergalactic Spacewar Olympics received bragging rights and a yearlong subscription to *Rolling Stone* magazine. Compared to today's multi-million-dollar prizes, that doesn't seem like much!

Young gamers compete to win the National Space Invaders Championship in 1981.

Internet Invasion

When the internet took off in the 1990s, it opened up a whole new world of competitive gaming. Gamers no longer had to sit in the same room to compete. They could now go online and battle each other across great distances. As the popularity of online play grew, companies began to **sponsor** video game world championships.

One of the first big competitions was the Red Annihilation Tournament in 1997. Players from across the United States competed in *Quake*, a **first-person** shooter game. In the finals Dennis "Thresh" Fong destroyed his competitor Tom "Entropy" Kimzey by a score of 14 to -1. Fong won $5,000 and was crowned the first official esports champion. Fong also won a custom Ferrari 328 GTS that belonged to John Carmack, a co-founder of id Software, which had published *Quake*.

first-person—a video game mode in which you see everything from the point of view of the character you are playing

sponsor—to provide money or equipment for a team or company in exchange for advertising

Fun Fact

Quake still draws many players to compete in frenzied combat. The updated version of the game, *Quake Champions*, is used in competitions today. Winners can take home prizes as high as $200,000.

Welcome to the Big Game

In recent years the popularity of esports has risen to an even higher level. **Streaming** platforms like Twitch.tv allow fans from around the world to watch live competitions. In 2013 Twitch viewers watched 12 billion minutes of gaming video per month. That averages out to 106 minutes per user every day! That year Twitch also reached an incredible 45 million viewers per month. The jump was partly due to the rise in popularity of broadcast esport competitions.

stream—to transfer data from one location to another through the internet

Esports fans enjoy gathering in large arenas and cheering on their favorite pro players and teams.

As interest has risen in esports, so has the size of the prizes. In 2017 more than 3,700 esports tournaments were held worldwide. More than $120 million dollars in prize money was given to the victors. There seems to be no end in sight. Money generated from esports competitions is expected to reach $1.5 billion by the year 2020!

Big Money

The highest prize at a single esports competition was $25.5 million dollars. The prize was awarded at The International 2018: Dota 2 Championships. The underdog team, OG (Europe) beat PSG.LSG (China) to take home the grand prize. The prize pool was funded by battle pass transactions. These in-game purchases allow players to buy new skins, weapons, and other items to enhance the game.

CHAPTER 3

Pro gamers focus on their tasks in the Overwatch eSports finals at the 2017 Zurich Game Show in Switzerland.

Professional Playgrounds

Overwatch League

One of today's most popular esports organizations is the Overwatch League (OWL). The league consists of 20 teams that are divided into two divisions. The OWL season begins in February and runs through August. The season is broken into four stages that each last five weeks. Teams play 28 matches during the season to determine who will go on to the Grand Finals.

Fun Fact

Overwatch League fans and players can buy digital "jerseys" for any of the playable heroes within the game. The money made from these in-game purchases goes to the league.

After the regular season concludes, the two division winners automatically get into the playoffs. The next four teams with the best records also move on to the playoffs. Two more **wild card** teams are determined through a play-in tournament. All eight of these teams then compete for the chance to play in the Grand Finals. The winner of the Grand Finals is crowned the Overwatch League Champion.

Overwatch League Divisions	
Pacific Division	Chengdu Hunters, Dallas Fuel, Guangzhou Charge, Hangzhou Spark, Los Angeles Gladiators, Los Angeles Valiant, San Francisco Shock, Seoul Dynasty, Shanghai Dragons, Vancouver Titans
Atlantic Division	Atlanta Reign, Boston Uprising, Florida Mayhem, Houston Outlaws, London Spitfire, New York Excelsior, Paris Eternal, Philadelphia Fusion, Toronto Defiant, Washington Justice

wild card—a team that advances to the playoffs even though it did not qualify for a playoff spot from its regular season record

Counter Strike Competitions

In 2000 the Electronic Sports League (ESL) was formed to coordinate worldwide events. Although the ESL runs tournaments for other games, *Counter Strike: Global Offensive* (or *CS:GO*) is easily the most popular competition. It's a huge game in the first-person esports arena.

CS:GO Major Championship Stages

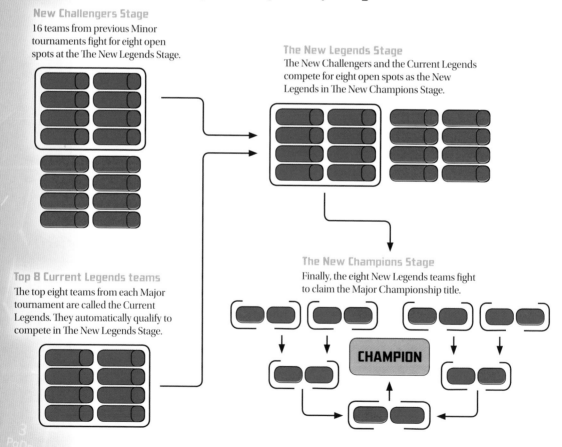

New Challengers Stage
16 teams from previous Minor tournaments fight for eight open spots at the The New Legends Stage.

The New Legends Stage
The New Challengers and the Current Legends compete for eight open spots as the New Legends in The New Champions Stage.

Top 8 Current Legends teams
The top eight teams from each Major tournament are called the Current Legends. They automatically qualify to compete in The New Legends Stage.

The New Champions Stage
Finally, the eight New Legends teams fight to claim the Major Championship title.

CHAMPION

⬤ ADVANCE TO NEXT BRACKET   ⬤ ELIMINATED   ◯ CHAMPION

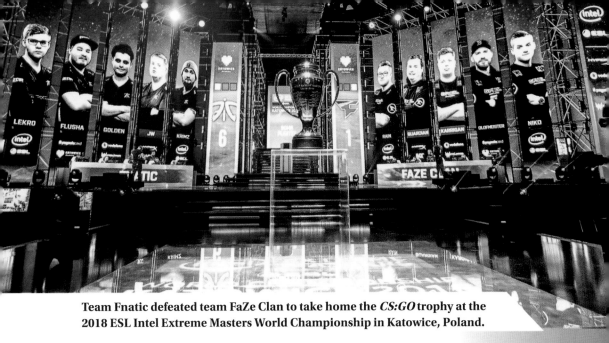

Team Fnatic defeated team FaZe Clan to take home the *CS:GO* trophy at the 2018 ESL Intel Extreme Masters World Championship in Katowice, Poland.

CS:GO tournament play differs from many esports competitions. Any team can join Minor competitions around the world and compete to **qualify** as a New Challenger for the Major Championship tournament. The top teams from the Major tournaments, known as the Current Legends, automatically qualify. They battle the New Challengers to move on to the New Champions Stage. There, the eight remaining teams compete for the title. The winner of the Major Championship tournament is crowned the world's best *CS:GO* team.

Fun Fact

In 1999 the original *Counter Strike* game was released as a variation of the legendary game *Half-Life*. Since then the game evolved into its own series and has become one of the biggest and most popular esports titles around.

qualify—to earn a starting spot in a race by completing timed laps

More than 11,000 fans filled the arena to watch the London Spitfires take on the Philadelphia Fusion at the 2018 Overwatch League Grand Finals in Brooklyn, New York.

Esports Explosion

Not too long ago, players got their game on by gathering in a friend's basement. They'd sit on the couch and battle each other on a single computer or gaming console. But today's biggest games have grown into a worldwide sensation. Thousands of fans pack giant arenas while millions of viewers watch the tournaments from their homes. Along with bragging rights, victors also win cash prizes worth millions of dollars.

Esports is a multi-million dollar business. In 2018 esports leagues made more than $905 million dollars and had 380 million viewers. Video game companies have jumped at the chance to earn part of that money. Game series such as Call of Duty, Gears of War, Rainbow Six, Halo, and others have been incredibly profitable. Game companies sell millions of copies of their games around the world. They also make a lot of money at esports tournaments from game sponsors and ticket sales.

TOP ESPORT GAME PRIZE MONEY*

	Amount	Players	Tournaments
Dota 2	$177,665,705	2,927	1,086
Counter-strike: Global Offensive	$74,170,609	11,495	3,997
League of Legends	$64,778,534	6,153	2,215
Starcraft II	$29,961,361	1,900	5,321
Fortnite	$24,591,992	2,224	271

* numbers current as of April 2019

Esport teams need to practice many hours together to learn teamwork and communication skills within the game.

Playing at Work

A Job with Joysticks

Just like professional athletes, esport gamers have to train for the big competitions. While esports might seem like they're all fun and games, pro players often have a grueling schedule. Some gamers train for most of the day. They must be alert and have quick reflexes to stay at the top of their game. If they don't train regularly, player performances can suffer. And if gamers aren't in top form, their coaches can send them to the bench.

Coaching the Team

Every esports team needs a good coach. Coaches study the players' strengths and weaknesses to decide who is best for each of the game's roles. They often run defensive and offensive drills for the team to practice. Coaches also study arena maps to find the best positions for the players. Like any good football or basketball coach, an esports coach will review video of the opponents' gameplay. This allows the coach to find strategies to give the team the best chance to win.

nutritionist—a person who studies nutrition and suggests ways to eat well

Training Together

Top esports players come from all over the world. To be successful, it's important for a team to train together regularly. To make that easier, some teams use special training facilities. Players can literally live and train together during the course of the season. These gaming **compounds** usually have sleeping quarters, kitchens, and meeting rooms. And of course, they have special gaming rooms for players to sharpen their skills.

compound—a group of buildings or rooms used for a common purpose

Many esports players live, eat, and sleep in the same building so they can train with their teammates more easily during the gaming season.

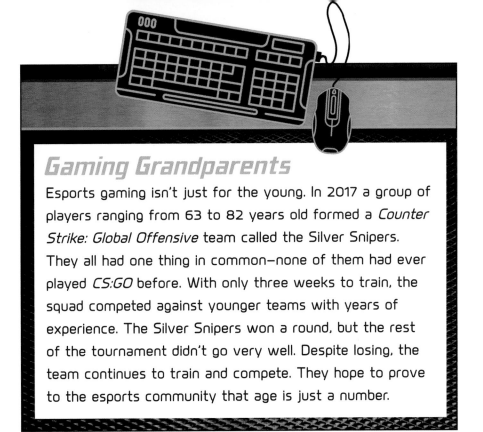

Gaming Grandparents

Esports gaming isn't just for the young. In 2017 a group of players ranging from 63 to 82 years old formed a *Counter Strike: Global Offensive* team called the Silver Snipers. They all had one thing in common—none of them had ever played *CS:GO* before. With only three weeks to train, the squad competed against younger teams with years of experience. The Silver Snipers won a round, but the rest of the tournament didn't go very well. Despite losing, the team continues to train and compete. They hope to prove to the esports community that age is just a number.

Training during an esports season can be intense. For up to five months, players are expected to train for 12 hours a day, six days a week. However, there are rewards to playing video games for a living. Pro esports gamers can expect to make about $60,000 a year. On top of that, sponsors often pay them to use their products such as gaming keyboards and energy drinks. And of course, winning an esports championship can result in a million-dollar payday!

CHAPTER 5

Not All Fun and Games

Erasing Racism in Esports

Over the years, esports competitions have seen incredible growth in popularity. Millions of fans all over the world enjoy watching their favorite games and cheering on their favorite players. However, most pro esports gamers seem to be young white or Asian men. There don't seem to be many black or Latino players. Why is this?

There may be a very negative reason why there are few gamers of color. Many die-hard gamers play only on high-end personal computers, or PCs. Some of these people like to call themselves the "PC Master Race." This phrase has clear racist tones to it that many people find offensive.

And sadly, sometimes people get carried away and tend to make racist comments during the heat of competition. However, the pro gaming leagues are working to remove the "trolls" and toxic words of racist fans and players. Abusive users who post offensive comments online are being blocked and locked out of the message boards. Pro players who get out of line can also be fined and instantly **disqualified** from competition.

Fun Fact

Tournaments for computer-based games tend to have larger prizes than console-based games. The 2018 International Dota 2 Championships had a prize pool of nearly $25 million. But a *Street Fighter V* competition's top prize was just $100,000.

disqualify—to prevent someone from taking part in an activity because he or she broke the rules

Gender Neutral Gaming

Problems in the esports community don't end with racist attitudes. Female players have experienced verbal abuse and threats as well. Although video games have long been viewed as a male-dominated activity, today nearly half of all home gamers are female. Some pro tournaments have been organized to try to draw more women into the sport. The hope is that game fans will realize that female players are just as skilled as males.

Ksenia vilga Kluenkova plays an intense game of _Counter Strike: Global Offensive_ in Moscow, Russia.

AnneMunition celebrates a big win in *Call of Duty: Black Ops 4* at TwitchCon 2018 in San Jose, California.

There is also a big difference between male and female gamers when it comes to earnings. On average, male players make more than 700 percent more money than women. A large part of this huge pay gap is due to the large number of men playing in pro leagues. But even comparing the top earners side-by-side shows a big difference between men and women. Esport leagues hope this pay gap will be reduced as more women find success as pro gamers.

Fun Fact

Kim "Geguri" Se-yeon was the first female gamer to join an Overwatch APEX team.

Going for the Gold

Esports competitions have become a worldwide sensation. The sport draws millions of fans around the globe and creates nearly a billion dollars in **revenue** every year. It's safe to say that esports are here to stay.

The future of esports starts with today's generation. Some high schools are beginning to organize esports leagues for students interested in competing. The National Federation of State High Schools (NFHS) encourages students to participate in several competitive games.

Fun Fact

People may one day be able to watch esports at the Olympics! Officials are considering the possibility of including video games in the Olympic Games. But some people feel that video games have no place in the cherished sporting event.

revenue—the money that is made by a business

Think you're ready for the big leagues? Want to win a championship and claim the big prizes? Then grab your controller or keyboard and start training. Because when it comes to wrist-cramping, finger-blistering action, only the best will take home the trophy!

Glossary

compound (KAHM-pound)—a group of buildings or rooms used for a common purpose

disqualify (dis-KWAHL-uh-fy)—to prevent someone from taking part in an activity because he or she broke the rules

first-person (FURST PER-suhn)—a video game mode in which you see everything from the point of view of the character you are playing

medic (MED-ik)—a soldier trained to give medical help in an emergency or during a battle

nutritionist (noo-TRISH-uh-nist)—a person who studies nutrition and suggests ways to eat well

qualify (KWAHL-uh-fye)—to earn a starting spot in a race by completing timed laps

revenue (REV-uh-noo)—the money that is made by a business

sniper (SNY-pur)—a soldier trained to shoot at long-distance targets from a hidden place

sponsor (SPON-sur)—to provide money or equipment for a team or company in exchange for advertising

stream (STREEM)—to transfer data from one location to another through the internet

wild card (WILD CARD)—a team that advances to the playoffs even though it did not qualify for a playoff spot from its regular season record

Read More

Kaplan, Arie. *The Epic Evolution of Video Games*. Games and Gamers. Minneapolis: Lerner Publications Company, 2014.

Paris, David and Stephanie Herweck. *History of Video Games*. Huntington Beach, CA: Teacher Created Materials, 2017.

Troupe, Thomas Kingsley. *Battle Zone: The Inspiring Truth Behind Popular Combat Video Games*. Video Games vs. Reality. North Mankato, MN: Capstone Press, 2018.

Internet Sites

Super League
https://www.superleague.com/

ESPN: Esports
http://www.espn.com/esports/

Esports Earnings
https://www.esportsearnings.com/

Index